Forcing the Narcissus

By Susan Musgrave

Forcing
the
Narcissus

poems by

Susan Musgrave

M&S

Canadian Cataloguing in Publication Data

Musgrave, Susan, 1951–
    Forcing the narcissus

Poems.
ISBN 0-7710-6659-7

I. Title.

PS8576.U7F67   1994   C811'.54   C93-095224-3
PR9199.3.M87F67   1994

The publishers acknowledge the support of the Ontario Arts Council and the Canada Council for their publishing program.

Set in Joanna by The Typeworks, Vancouver

Printed and bound in Canada on acid-free paper.

McClelland & Stewart Inc.
The Canadian Publishers
481 University Avenue
Toronto, Ontario
M5G 2E9

1   2   3   4   5   98   97   96   95   94

Contents

IN THE SMALL HOURS OF THE RAIN

THE WET HEART OF THE WOUND

"Show me a single wound on earth that love has healed."

– Jim Harrison
Selected Poems

THE GIFT

In the beginning when your heart wants
to sing "Wild Thing," she turns up
the chamber music and from that point
you won't sleep. She shoots you
full of heroin, Southern Comfort,
her boyfriend's marigold-smelling prick.

When your nerves are half-formed
she takes you shopping for the weapons
you will need to survive with. You play
Baby Roulette, spitting cartridges faster
than bone cells replace cartilage. You don't
need a whole brain to know the word for hate
in all languages. You understand love
is something that needs to be cut off
like the umbilicus, though there's no knife
long enough to sever your bodies for good.

Before your eyes have opened you know
your childhood belongs to someone else,
a connection who crosses the placenta

and makes your heartbeat wilder than ever.
Heart forming four chambers, vocal cords
complete. You try crying out against
the requiems your mother makes you
listen to, but it's too late now

she has decided to keep you and you feel
her reaching to stitch it up, the sad
equipment of womanhood. You want to console
her, forgive her, for this is her first
experience, and no one has taught her how
to sew. Her bloody fingers poke around
for you, they could hurt you

but before your lips have learned to say
leave me alone you have remembered
you can sing. You sing "Happy Birthday"
until she begins to push. Singing
won't help later when she tries to flush
your crushed head down a public toilet
but it helps you now, moments before
your head is engaged, held still and quiet
in the basin of your mother's bones. Singing

seems to be a kind of salvation. You know
every song about Hell and what to expect
when you get there. Now you're howling your way

down the birth canal, past empty gin bottles,
used syringes. After nine months of happiness
you're learning withdrawal, what it's like to be
fully human, how your mother only gives you
all she's got to give.

THE WET HEART OF THE WOUND

When I began to have a body
where were you? As I grew into a young girl
waving goodbye, you were in some room
weeping for the life you'd already left behind,
a room emptier than a limousine
that pulled in off the highway
and left you under the VACANCY sign.

When you loosened the knot in your tie
and switched on the TV, I was the one
in the silent movie who stood in the doorway,
waiting. I was working to get my lipstick right
when a stranger with your father's eyes
began to work over the body of the one
who had betrayed him. I was the one

the stranger slapped so hard it knocked you
to the ground, so hard you heard your father
howling in the night, saw a human stool
thick as a soup tin in the jammed toilet

as you tried to get back to your mother's
womb, to the wet heart of the wound.

You'd seen me somewhere before. But when
that stranger touched his thick cock to my lips,
and my wild eyes looked around for you,
there was nothing you could do but remember.

And it was like remembering your daughter,
as if you were the one pumping into her
smearing bright lipstick at the edges of her mouth.

And it was as if you were my father
and I, finally brave enough, had come home.

MY FATHER CAME BACK FOR THE FURNITURE

and now he's in the bathtub
where my mother is trying to drown him.
She holds him down by the ankles
while he does a back-stroke rapidly.

In real life he was good
at the breast-stroke. Something is wrong
and my father has an erection
for the first time since 1956,
the year I was conceived if I am
to believe in anything.

I'm embarrassed by what I see.
Later when, without dignity, he's floating
with my sister's bath-toys beached on him
I think, "He has lived." That's all,
there are no other words for it,
nothing to say how degrading death is,
and all the more so for its pettiness.

My mother remains calm and picks up
her knitting. She's making a pair of sleepers
for the baby she'll never bear.

My sister puts her feet on the coffee table
and weeps. I go out the back door and squat
beside a garbage can to piss. When the stray
dog stops to sniff I kick him until he's sick.
I'm so heartless it would take a stone
to break me, my mother says. She doesn't
drop a stitch. Blesses our home.

ELEGY

It happened in a house I love;
my mother came to me carrying a cradle
with a child's body in it. I watched
how she kissed it and caressed it
as if it were her own daughter.

Then my mother placed the cradle
under the clock that stopped
years ago when I first stopped being
her daughter. I learned to tell time
by my father's lonely silences as he sat
hating the world we lived in.

In the house I loved I learned to hate, also,
the wind all around, the smell of candles burning.
I remember, too, the granite slabs my father
hauled home and laid out for our new summer
patio. They were ancient gravestones and I was
afraid to cross over them into the shade

but what panicked me more was having to sit
in that shade with my father, drawing up

plans for the afterworld. So I went into my own
world, conjuring spirits. My mother said nothing
when ghosts choked her hardy annuals, stunted
her gentle perennials. She poured tea
for my father who sat under the dying willow
as it rubbed against the roof and made our house
dangerous to live in.

When my daughter was born in the same house,
years later, her eyes were already ancient.
Time began again and I felt less lonely,
as if I could live in the world from then on
and know what I might expect from it.

Now my mother lights a candle
and the wind carries the light away.
The wind hauls an empty cradle away.

YOU COULD UNDERSTAND THIS

for Marion Quednau

I'm reading your book, the part
where your mother's life being too much
for him, your father takes a gun
from the trunk of the car and empties it
in her head, and she dies slowly, then he
shoots himself and that's only the beginning
of the first chapter

when suddenly I hear crying
at the front door and I look up
and it's my own parents standing there,
pleading with me to let them come in.

For thirty-five years I've been unable
to let them in. Come in
I say to my father, who loved the sea.
Come in I say to my mother
who looks like me.

And then – after all those years –
I don't know what else to say to them.

You could understand this.
So I look at my mother and say, "How's
it been?" And my mother replies only,
"He's going to leave me, finally."

I look at my father. "She says she wants me
to go," he whispers.
                        After all those years
your mother wants her life back

and suddenly you understand
your father. Forgive him. And then the world
stops, with tears on its young face.
The world comes to an end.
Or it just keeps on.

WHEN THE WORLD IS NOT OUR HOME

Once we returned to my father's house,
the house he had lived in as a child.
He said he found it unchanged, yet
when I looked at his face I felt
it must have changed. He died just the same,
as if he had been caught scheming

to live forever. That day we walked back
into the breathing fields, the same fields
his own father had planted. And when he stooped
to strip an ear of corn from its cornsilk sheaf
I remember how I blushed, afraid
he would be accused of stealing. I was
much younger then, and always afraid

of losing him. That day, too, we went to see
the family graves. The new owners said
they didn't mind if we stayed all day.
The graves looked abandoned and I wanted
to plant something that would grow there
forever, wild things to rise out of our graveyard
like late-blooming stars. My father had brought

tea, which we drank on my grandmother's
fallen headstone. He said she was fey
in the old days, and told people's fortunes
under the giant medlar. I wanted to be
her way, and studied the leaves on the bottom
of my tea cup until my father took the empty
cup away. I saw him, breathless, going

into the ground that day. Unable to bear
the way his face accused, I was changed
by loss, also. But looking back
over that day, I miss more now.

THE LAST THING

I was in Fredericton when you went
into a coma the last time, asleep
with some new stranger beside me.

The last thing you said to me
before I left was *how long will you be
gone?* I don't know I said, and from Fredericton
phoned home to see if you had forgiven me
for leaving. *I love you* I tried to say
over the long distance, then my mother
came on the line. I knew you wouldn't
speak to me because you had nothing left
that would give me anything to hang on to.

Then the line went dead.
And then you died and I didn't know who
was to blame for it.

FAMILY PLOT

1

It begins with a lump in the throat,
a sense of wrong, a homesickness,
it's never a thought to begin with
One slap and the pain comes back
calling itself love or discipline.

I never saw my father cry, never
saw him naked or smiling. I saw him
waving goodbye, for years I watched
him wave until one day it was my turn
to go somewhere finally.

How could I push past him
on his way to the grave? I'd already
died first, many times before him.
Now, at a ceremony he would have
grown impatient with already,
I listen to his brother reminisce
about their own childhood.

One time my grandfather caught
my father writing poetry. He made him
strip and go upstairs to think
about it *it's never a thought*
to begin with, it begins with
a sense of wrong then beat him
until my uncle didn't recognize him.

Another time he found my father
playing the baby grand. That time,
my uncle tells us, he broke
both his hands.

When my grandfather died we planted
forget-me-nots on his grave. "In many ways
he was a fair man," my uncle remembers;
in death we buried him deep so that
when the time came my father could join him
in the same plot. Now the time's come
and I'm unable to bury either of them
deep enough.

It begins with a lump in the throat,
a lovesickness, then I'm a child
again, I'm that naked. How pure
can the memory of violence be, how unbreakable
the habit of breaking? Once more
my father asks if I'm ready for more

though I'm old enough to know
this is the only life I have.

2

We're at my father's grave
planting flowers that won't last
the season. My daughter, aged three,
says if we dig far enough and move
all the earth he might come up again
before summer.

I watch as she picks up a handful
of dirt. For her this is an ordinary
experience. Come on I'll show you she says
when I stop, kneeling there
over a hole in the ground, not wanting
to go deeper than we already have, afraid
to drive the shovel home.

SOMETHING HAS TO GIVE IN A LIFE

"The dead watch us with a terrible caring."

– Carolyn See
Making History

FORCING THE NARCISSUS

I show him what he doesn't want
to see – love is a blind man
playing dice in a blizzard.

He swears these bright flowers
like words when cut will sing or bleed;
I believe he is only grieving
or that grief has a lot to do with it.
Blindness or too much brightness can be
the same thing. He says he wants to see the world
but lacks the simple means of getting there.

I tell him what he doesn't want
to hear – how I woke to find my father
forcing the tears that hung on my eyelashes
like wet gravel, how I felt the wind through
my rice paper door. How can I tell him life is less

than he imagines it to be, at the same time more
tangible than anything we know? It is
hard to believe plump bulbs sucked dry

as an old man's testicles will ever sing
or amount to very much. I carry them in
out of the ice-storm to the calm centre
of my father's room where, I'm told,
anything might bloom, it's no sin
to be surprised. In us grows the strange
and the wild barely covered by skin
yet I think how much thinner
is the membrane between myself and the world.

HISTORY LESSON

The child is dancing. It's all
she can do now that her mother lies
face down in the weeds and her father's
teeth have been broken like the small-paned
windows in the home they'd made together
on the outskirts of a town. Her parents

were ordinary people tending their garden
when the terrorists arrived. How tame
that garden might have grown
if it hadn't been for desire!

The man watching from the balcony next door
takes an historical overview.
He believes terrorism is the rage
of the literati in its final stage.
He's seen so many people exterminated
he's beginning to feel experienced.

The child stares up at the man.
To her he has always been ordinary

too – someone to be avoided, maybe
even feared. But now his interest
in her makes her nipples grow hard
and she's able to see her distant
former life as it could have been,
without pain, and it makes her feel
the rage of every grown-up woman.

She cuts new lips from her mother's
face and paints some lipstick on.
She makes a smile from her father's
teeth and puts it on, and history
moves on, too, in the rearview
mirror of the car she's driving away
into the future. There's one more dead
body in the trunk of the car, whose
it is she doesn't know yet.

The man sees through all these
stages. It's any suburban street
on any weekday morning and the school bus
hasn't arrived. Maybe there's no school
today, no lessons.

The man has seen history repeated
and still he'd like to see more.

He wants there to be much more than just
his ex-wife driving into the future
with their only child in the trunk of the car,
the child who, moments ago, tried dancing.

IMAGINE

a ten-year-old boy going to the park
armed with his father's rifle.
It's dark, it's the dead of summer
and he's come to pick off a few ducks,
the kind used to being kept
who won't be missed by anyone. The boy
takes his little sister with him.

His father has shown him how
to use the gun. "Imagine," the father says,
"there's a killer in front of you.
This gun is all you have." The boy
has sighted the ducks from his bedroom
window. All week he's been waiting
and when the right moment comes

he takes his little sister
to be his decoy. She loves ducks
though he's forgotten she's not old enough
to know you have to sneak up on them.

He wants his first shot to be true
like the kisses of his mother who thinks
her children are already safely sleeping.
He has deceived her before and she might
forgive him again this time

if he's resourceful. He raises his father's
sniper rifle towards the spectre of his
little sister running. She goes flying
towards the birds, crying
"Bang!" to the killer inside him.

RECEIVING END OF LOVE

You've been told you have a nose that can
sniff out the bad in any man, a heart
vacant as twin beds at the Paradise Motel.
You've been rode hard and put away wet
so many times now, at first

you feel useless, being on the receiving
end of love. At first there's nothing left
but the desire to make the best of it;
on a back lot in a strip of light
you join your names in blood.
But when his hand slips and he unloads
the machine-gun in your head,
you're forever his.

At first you feel an awful lot
is happening and then you get
desperate, not knowing if it's happiness,
until one night on a trick
bed he ties your wrists to the posts
and slips a coin between your lips. You flip

it twice on your tongue, sucking
this big spender into your back pocket right
where you always wanted him –

and then you get down, shaking
your hips in memory of a rhythm
you once lived your life to, making it.

EFFORT OF LOVE

Coincidence, you say, if traced
back far enough, becomes inevitable.
In the Zen Restaurant you ask for the menu
though a sign tells us *there is nothing*
to eat, there is nothing to drink,
there is only history. I take this
as inevitable until our waiter arrives.

You order wings, to begin with.
Beneath your clothes your body keeps
its distance, empty of anything
resembling love. I draw you deep
into my brain and have sex with you
there. I stay hungry this way
but when I look at your eyes I see
you have finished eating. Now the waiter

moves a child's chair to our table,
brings clean plates. Our last course
has taken a lifetime of preparation,
the chef tells us; it's an effort of love.

Before us the history of cruelty
is repeated. The chef straps his still
living creation in the child's seat and we see
the spirit is weak; the body weeps
with the pain of understanding so little

but offers no resistance. "The absence
of effort is a characteristic of great vigour,"
our chef says, as he cracks the skull open
and pours hot oil into the still
thinking head.

"To love," you whisper, digging deep
in the brain. What makes human beings
forgive one another?

See how our creature closes her eyes.
Her tears grow old on the bone-white plates.

THE SPIRITUALIZATION OF CRUELTY

The night it snowed a man set fire
to his dog near the road. Chained him
to a stake by a pile of burning timber,
a blind dog who would not have believed
such brightness possible.

The villagers came to watch, to warm
themselves at the bonfire. One who was known
to have a way with animals talked about
the cruelty of having to keep a dog tied up.

Beyond the road a woman lay naked
in the first snow. They had tied her legs
open under the crude shelter of the spruce
where they took turns fucking her with the
femur of a pig. But when she wouldn't
shut her eyes as her baby buckled and kicked

they cut out her eyes and buried them deep
inside her. Then the one who had never had
a fighting woman fucked her hard in the black

holes of her face before wiping himself
in her red hair and reeling back to the road
where the heat was beginning to enter
the dog's bones and the man who was known
to have a way with animals started kicking
the fire out.

A waning moon, like a breast that lays
itself bare against a child's face, rose
over the snow, and the spaces between stars
grew brighter. The child does not know
almost everything we call art is
the spiritualization of cruelty. She sees
only through the eyes of a naked woman
painting the stars out in the lonely
new silence of her future, as if all
the brilliance she had been reaching for
was in blindness.

IN THE SHADE OF THE MEMORIAL

there lay a goat. I sat in the sun
with an old man who sold replicas
of the crucifix, and flowers he laid out
on a torn gravecloth, and oranges.

Children carried sacks of offal
out of the grove, and a sorcerer wrapped
a double rainbow in his rags. I hacked
blood into the beggar's cup as he passed,
a chipped cup with two black teeth at the bottom.

The beggar cried "The dead have risen!
The dead have risen!" and two guinea-fowl
who had escaped from the market
messed themselves in front of the memorial.
Secretly I was glad. Secretly I had been waiting
for something like this to happen.

Both were dazed, both were bleeding as they
teetered in the shade of the memorial where
the goat was lying. One tried to peck out

the goat's closed eye. The goat didn't move
and I thought *these are our times.*

Later in a room, both of us wanting
everything to be over, I dragged my tongue,
leaving a blood-trail from your legs and belly
to your mouth.

THIS FAR SOUTH

We were lost in the lazy ways people become
lost. He said I want you but it was the drink
speaking. Then last night he caved his
mother's head in with a gun I saw him
steal from her lover's glove compartment.

I'm taking the word innocence
out of the language. In forever, he said,
I found no justice.

We put his mother's head in the trunk
and spun it all over Los Angeles. Her dog
kept clawing to get in at it. Makes you
sick to think.

I need you, he said, but in the heat
I took the gun and emptied it. Still I can weep
thinking how he could play the concertina.

He wanted to be with me forever, he said,
but I knew they'd catch up to us

sooner. I'll tell the judge, in my innocence
I found no justice. Maybe he'll have mercy
but I doubt it.

This far south the mind can spin
like a silver-plated revolver in the wrong
hands. When the sun shines down, it

really shines.

SOMETHING HAS TO GIVE IN A LIFE

Last night I took a gun
and fired it at something, maybe you.
Afterwards, after the silence,
there was a hole as big as my heart
and the light shone through.

I keep trying to believe in pain
because pain, like love,
so easily mystified, holds true.

We woke the baby with our singing
and crying. Her heartbeat was something
always to be remembered, something
to love forever.

ONE EVENING, THE WIND RISING, IT BEGAN

raining. I peeked out from behind the blinds
while the lights blinked and my mother went
from room to room in her silence, lighting the
few candles. Flowers on their drunken stems
were opening themselves like brides, and I tried
to explain to my daughter how she couldn't go out
and play any longer in that garden.

Tears fell like spring rain down her face
when I said I thought death might be something
we could return from as another life.
She didn't want to hear this and pushed me
away. She said she wanted to be herself,
always. She wanted me, too, to be who I am.

I have reached an age when even a spring
rain falling on spring ground can make me
less of what I am. So I told her then what I've tried
to believe in my life, that we don't have to die,
ever. Victorious she turned to me, like the flowers
of this world, the brilliance sliding from her.

WHERE HE LIVES

In the room where you sleep you take the postcard
your father sent from the country where he lives
and hold it under your night-light as if
light could bring him closer and be his awakening.

What can I tell you? What you see is true,
a woman wades naked into the sea and to you
she looks beautiful, to you it seems
natural. The waves make no sound breaking up
on the shore and you are not to know this
naked beautiful woman is sad and usual underneath.

I turn out your light because we dream
deeper in darkness, and mourn you all night as if
suddenly you are not there any more, as if
you are left with no one.

MY GIRL IS ENTERING THE FIRST GRADE

We're late, the car has engine problems
and the temperature outside is
falling. My daughter wants to know
how life begins. I pump the gas, hoping
for another miracle.

Our grown cats loll on the lawn, some
innocent pink thing between them
giving its final whimper. I shout
at the cats who slouch towards the vacant
lot next door as my father opens the door
and steps out into the cold. He won't

last another winter but he doesn't know
it yet. I wave him back inside to keep
warm at the first fire he's had to build
this season. Bone-coloured smoke rises
straight into the air; the engine turns

over and I back out on the road. My girl
wants to know why we need to grow old,
as I drive her away from me
towards her first day alone.

IN THE SMALL HOURS OF THE RAIN

"Western wind, when wilt thou blow?
The small rain down can rain.
Christ, that my love were in my arms,
And I in my bed again."

– Anon

POSSIBILITIES

Purple vetch and wild roses
mark the edge of the clearing
where you in a white robe bend
over a green bowl sinking your face
in rain. Foxgloves and blue
lupine reach for the sky
where the stars are lined up
like targets you could have
picked off blindfolded.

"There are possibilities for me, but
under what stone, beloved, do they lie?"
I heard my mother's cradle song
the first time I undid my dress
for you in the cemetery, and squatted
without panties, in stinging nettles
over my father's grave to show
how far I'd go. The pain excited me
because of the possibilities
because of what could happen

if you once sunk your face
into my white breasts or rubbed
cool mint leaves between my thighs.

Now I know where our possibilities lie

coming back to you this last time
with day breaking. I gather
Queen Anne's Lace for the table
beside your bed, and Mock Orange
white as the morphine you take
every odd hour for pain. In my life
I've made choices, now I've come to you
the whole distance. From our window I see

wild strawberries, like hearts,
swelling amongst mint leaves.

THE SMALL NIGHT SO ALONE OUT THERE

Down on my knees in this
lost motel room, your voice
telling me *take it come on*,
knowing there are no limits
only the cool night coming on.

I take you into me, my heart
a wilder place than all the world
beyond. It's never been so easy
in any other motel room. You're hard
and I work you like a woman
who knows she is inexhaustible.

I won't stop; I want to keep you this way
because this way I'm sure of you.
I've got nothing on but the stockings
you gave me and they keep coming down.
You don't care, you just say *take it all*
come on.

But I always wanted it to last with you;
my hands, my lips became something

closer to water. I wanted to give it all,
down on my knees, my thin dress, the one
you liked me to wear, lying lonely where I'd
stepped from it, small ghost in a doorway.

Afterwards you press yourself into me,
over my breasts until my nipples get hard,
and between my legs. Laying me back,
it fits you say to me then. *Feel*
how it fits in there.

TONIGHT AT SUNRISE

*"But then everything else stops
because I don't know what happens after that."*
  – Linda Gregg

You were on a roll.
There was bad weather behind you
and a good woman waiting
and the whole world was singing
of the day it was born.

You were going for broke, going down
alone. I was in a room writing poetry
for someone I loved and I didn't know then
the road you were on.

If I'd known I would have come to you
with this light around my body.
Made an effort to come towards you:
can you imagine the kind of emptiness
I've grown used to?

It's like someone in the same room telling
a joke that's on you.
You don't understand the punch-line.
You laugh anyway.

SNOWSTORM IN THE DESERT

We're all alone out here. I love
you like I love the stars, and the
black branches the stars hang on,
and the trees that huddle together
in a brightness we never dreamed of.

I was like that once. I mean, a girl
huddling under a waste of sky.
I used to walk out over the burning
sand and feel nothing, but now
my feet are ancient and scarred.
You say you want a body that's been
lived in, used. Well, I've lived
alone that way.

See these breasts. They are ringed
with the marks the wind leaves.
I've lived longer than the desert air
where you've dipped your tongue into me,
flicked it over, licked and
teased the darkness out of me.

It's winter and your lips taste of me.
You throw your head back and open your
mouth wide and I watch the first snowflakes
settle onto your tongue. There's nothing,
nothing better. You truly know that.

And grind into me, hard, until the sand
underneath is crying for us to stop. We can't
stop – there's no stopping it. Cold
sand and snow burning through
to the core. We have to tough it out.

RAZOR-WIRE, MILLHAVEN PENITENTIARY

It slices through my heart
the way it surrounds you,
and something the colour of blood
spills out. In so much blackness
the heart leaps, jumps a beat
by the wall, goes over.

You've slashed your hands on the wind,
your eyes on a woman's body,
but nothing, not even the stars going out,
has hurt as much as this.

The heart is a gash
and the sky glitters, but all
that high wire coiled and ready to cut
can't keep tenderness out.

The distance between us
is the thickness of blood. Love
jumps away, jumps
out of us.

AFTER WORDS

The world came to an end last night
and you weren't with me. The same wind
that always sulks around the house
plucked up the pages of the letter
I was writing and carried them away.

When I told you my dream where you were
leaving me forever, it got caught in the weeping
willow and hung there becoming
part of the devastation. I had wanted
to tell you why I made love
to a rain-maker in a previous existence,
and a snake-charmer who called me baby love
then wept for the woman he'd betrayed –

but how little they meant to me! I thought
only of you as I brushed the taste of rain
from my tongue and made a love charm
out of spit and an image of you bending
to enter me. I want you. I want you to know
I've written to you, faithfully. But even when

I send silence the wind tears through it
so the simple words I use fragment
and become unreadable. "I love you,"
I must have written, over and over,
though piecing it together afterwards
it was as if somebody else had written it.

offer little. Earth and rocks
and black black emptiness
reverse any prayers I might have
had in me. Alone under the bluffs
I still think a life is possible.
Like panic or immediate fear,
I still believe love holds something.

In the visiting room we just
hold on. A guard gulps
ice-water on the other side of the glass.
Your hands are torn and I am naked,
trussed up in the dirt like a wild thing
no one can tame. But you tried.
"I only wanted to love you," I cry.

You cry, too, for the wounds closing over.
It's metaphor, of course, or a bad dream
where we only use love to hurt each other.
It's a risk to feel anything here, inside.

We're both prisoners, guarded. We look at the
mountains but we know we're not going
anywhere. Because there's nowhere

to go. You climb rocks and earth,
out of breath into emptiness,
and when you get to the top you have to
start back down.

IN THE SMALL HOURS OF THE RAIN

"Sorrow is a nourishment forever."
   – Carolyn Kizer

I'm leaving again
and Stephen's sad-night eyes
fill the darkness. Behind his eyes
the world's pain becomes
something I'm grateful for,
something tried but unpredictable
that darts into the heart and leaves
its ragged truth there.

I've got scars to prove it.
I've never belonged to anyone.
Now his eyes fill that emptiness
with something beyond love
and I can't get enough of it;
like grief, there's never enough.

"HERE IT COMES —
GRIEF'S BEAUTIFUL BLOW-JOB"

– William Matthews

Last night for the first time
you told me you loved me less.
I put on a child's dress, pinned
a half-moon to my breast and walked
uptown. The streetlamps kept on
whispering of you as I waited
for one who would love me anyway.

How little it takes to mend, how little
to break. The first man who gave me a ride
had a valentine the colour of blood
under his shirt. He took me for a drive down
the wrong side of the road playing
"Here Comes the Night" so loud I didn't
even hear the real night come crashing
in on me the way it did. Dress of gauze
over my right eye, two fist-shaped moons
under my left. He left me for dead
but it didn't even hurt —

not the way it hurt to be
loved less.

Motif of passion-flowers at the HooDoo Motel,
the kitchen comes fully equipped, the bed
has Magic Fingers. Everything but my heart comes
equipped. The philosopher in the bomber jacket
who says, "'No' means bondage, bitch,"
he's equipped. He's a realist. He had a real
whip. He gave me everything except a rag
to wipe the blood up with. He made me strip

then took his realistic jiggler out
and told me there was no one cause
for any human act of degradation.
I'd thought no one could touch me
when it came to self-abuse until he had me
licking my own blood off two cheap passion
flowers on the white lino

but nothing could have prepared me
for this, to be loved less.

When I was a child my father butchered
my first pet, a wild rabbit I'd tamed
and fed until she grew big enough to eat.
Then he killed her with his long hands
and dressed her and made me eat; every day
of my life he forced me to keep eating
until there was nothing left. It was a lesson
in sufficiency, he said.

But when you told me you loved me less,
I didn't know how to cure it.
The bed became smaller than cruelty
with just enough room for the two of us
and the night came over me
like a backhand over the mouth
like my father with steak blood
in the corner of his mouth
holding up a photograph of his
shy, wild daughter.

I wanted to give reasons why I tried to love you
more each day, but it all sounded
so ordinary, like taking a piece of bread
and cutting it. Even this simple act
brings a knife into play

so the moon packs her bags and moves
away. Not me, I'm here for the duration.
Grief's never had it so good.

LYING IN BED ALONE I HEAR YOU SAY

everything is over between us.
To our late visitor you whisper,
"but she must never know."

You kiss the dice for luck, toss them high
and your luck changes. Deep inside the house
our small daughters are sleeping
in an emptiness they cannot yet put a name to.
As a child I wanted to die because –
I believed then – nothing could be
more frightening than living.

In the next room I hear you laughing.
You embrace our friend, who one day
will be able to tell me she had never been
held so hungrily, then hug our daughters
and tuck them in to bed. I can feel your arms,
the way the muscles flex like soapstone clouds,
the ancient way they stretched out to me
the first time, earnest as beauty.

I remember, too, how I loved your skin,
tattoo of a spicy wind blowing its
redhot cinnamon heart out to meet my lips
and stick there like an unrepentant kiss.
And I loved your eyes, the pain in them
gentle as the scent of rain in a lemon grove

but you must never know how much
I will always be in love with you.
I who have been so capable of leaving, stay
awake until dawn, just long enough
to call it mourning.

LOVE WASN'T ALWAYS

You've been out back butchering
all week. I cleave the heart and fry
the last of the black boar in hog's grease
until his blood weeps. You like your piece
done so there's something for your teeth
to sink into. I watch you eat
and later, when you sleep, your body
smelling of jerked meat and the juice
that's been pent up in me all week,

I lie beside you thinking
love wasn't always this way with us.
"Ugly as love" you called the one sow
who wouldn't die quickly on the slab
the way you wanted her to, trusting you.

Love wasn't always this way. Sometimes
I thought it could last, like the first time
I came to you innocent as air

and you were waiting there.

STOPPING BY THE MAILBOX
ON A SNOWY EVENING

What could be more frightening
than living? Why didn't you take
a later boat to Vancouver?

Why couldn't we stay in bed
forever, smoke dope, talk dirty
and not try to change anything?

Why didn't we? Why?

ROLLING BOIL

" . . . oh, it's all so human and sad,
for money and love are terrible things
with which to fill all our human days
and nights, and nobody blames you much,
not even I, despite all the trouble I've had . . . "
– Robert Penn Warren

1

Last night in Los Angeles
while another woman made love to you
a rat fell into my toilet
and drowned. It really did.
You know I wouldn't exaggerate.

For every rat drowning
there is a person like me
letting one drown.
I closed the lid of the toilet,
called my closest friends in town.
I was much too late,
they were already sleeping

and you didn't answer either.
The despair I felt all day
hasn't caught up to me yet.
Not quite. Despair wears a sinker
around its heart and this is it, boys,
one more nameless heart goes down.

2

I went to war
and got wounded. I want to grieve
because of this?

I thought I'd done everything,
gone to the core where the claw
grips, but all I got was memories
when I tried to recall the past.

Pain makes a list.
It puts you at the top.
Puts you at the top and crosses you out.
You won't be missed. Not one bit.

Think of it.

3

I made love to you in every
position. Except the last position,
the one I keep coming back to.

Reloading your gun, you tell me
this is peace. You think your own life
is significant. You keep on giving me
reasons for death.

4

All summer I've been mistaken.
About you. I should have inscribed
on my body words like *I will love*
nothing forever instead of loving you
like this. It would have made more sense.

Everything hurts me.
The flowers in the garden,
the knives asleep in the drawer I keep
the silver in. Nothing stops screaming long
enough. Even the bedsprings make me think
of you, the way they nudge me, nightly,
into the dull anonymity of sleep.

I haven't slept well. I want to
kill something. My therapist asks,
seriously, "Are you angry?" All morning
I've been thinking how will I get back to you,
how will I, will.

5

I've had enough. I knew there'd be
a night when I'd say there's
nothing more.

My fingers curl and snarl
like stunned dogs. The ugliest
telephone in the world is silent.

We can't begin again.
I knew there'd come a time
when the water began to boil.
Trouble for you.
Trouble for you because when it
boils it burns.

6

Now is not the time for forgiveness,
not the place. My hands still shake
and I want you to call so I can let
you know I'm finally all right. I am,
of course. I couldn't be better. Except
if we were in bed together and all this
darkness were something kind like morphine
instead of sick, like love.

But love doesn't enter it.
It never did.

7

I don't need you now.
I dreamed of a perfect garden
where everything was frozen and white.
The blossoms on the trees
could have snapped if I'd touched them,
and the delicate spring flowers had lost
their beautiful colours. Dull cold
will do that.

I sipped tea with a Japanese.
Under his thin robe he had an erection
and that too was frozen. I slipped it
inside and it warmed in me.
I took the last drop of him
and brought it to you.

Try to understand.
I saw your face pressed cold
against the glass, a face full
of its own fear, hunted by something.

8

This is supposed to be love.
If you blink you might not feel it
but the effect is cumulative.

If you've only known one eye,
how can you miss another?
If the quick heart misses a beat
can life be otherwise than over?

In the wildness of your body I found,
for a time, a kind of peace. Small animals
with their eyes plucked out by birds and
hacked-off heads – these seemed like
minor distractions.

It's love all right. The way
gold changes in certain lights,
and promises are broken.

9

I am doing this to myself,
you say, but you have the power
to heal me.

Only you. There's a cracked bowl
with a head in it on your table
and two bloody plates
we are supposed to eat from.

We are equals, you say,
and split the head down the middle.
It occurs to me now
it's my head we are eating.

(You always told me, "You won't suffer."
For years, whole years, tears wouldn't come.)

10

At last you're on the phone saying
I should come down and see you,
let you kiss the wounded places,
but they are oozing, love,
it isn't pretty.

The stumps, the gouges – not
professional. You're no surgeon;
you think you can make me better?
I'm getting better without you.
Without you I am always better.

Love comes sad as fog, slow
as trust, and nobody blames you much,
not even I.

the way you do.
You're out to kill
the love in me, the alternatives
to living. Now I'm just waiting
for a look, a call.
I want details – how do you do it
that you do it so well?

Did you plan it or was it
spontaneous? I am no longer
identifiable. I'm an amputee.

You hacked your way in
and out of me.
Even my blood was turned off
at the source, you see
little by little you're using me
up. I'm almost empty, full
of this sad love.

So if I come back,
if I cross continents to see you
and you're not expecting me, remember –
for thirty-three years
it was the wind that took
the better part of me

and nobody gets over me
the way you do.
Not even you.

AS IF IT WASN'T

enough to leave me, you've come back.
I've been down at the river
gathering gravel and mud into my arms
and I saw the whole world passing me by,
and it didn't mean much.

You take me in your own arms
and try to comfort me.
You think a kiss, a caress,
can mend anything.
Listen, I've lived too long,
I'm lucky, look at my palms.

I'm a luxury and you know it.
You'd trade all the women
with their wet lips and their words,
you'd trade the feel of their
uncomplicated bodies

for a share of my loneliness,
because I own it.

You can't bear what I know.
And as if it isn't enough
you try to take me
as if I were whole and ordinary

but you don't like it after all,
the distances in me.

I suppose you'll leave.
I'm getting used to it
and it doesn't mean much.
I'm familiar with the easy way
it goes badly from the beginning
when the heart first closes itself to hope
like a tired woman stooping
to scoop the river up.

THIS IS THE DAY

I have nothing under my skirt
but a whole lot of lessons I never learned
properly. The man labouring on the road
senses that, and waves a fingerless hand
hoping for a quick throw over the lunch hour.

Your life isn't your own any more
when a man like that can bruise his eyes
on emptiness, and leave you wanting.
In a huff I move from the stoop

into the house where my friends have laid
a feast around my body. It's been dying
for days and they've dusted it
– "she would have wanted it that way" –
with cake flour to make it look ghostly.

I don't want it, who would want anything like it?
I fume around the place for awhile
but there is no outlet now, there never was.
It seems a shame to have loved a man so long
who was the wrong man

but suddenly there comes a day when I can move
through a room without you. And this
is the day.

MEETING YOU AGAIN

I don't know which fear rose in me
as we walked the frozen road through
Sudden Valley back to the hotel where we'd met
after a nine-month separation, to make
love all the long night, the same night
John Lennon died in New York.

I remember wearing your shoulder holster
to the door when room service came
with wild salmon from the Similkameen
and hot chocolate we spiked with *aguardiente*
you'd smuggled in your luggage from Colombia.
I wore, too, an antique Tibetan vest,
and my breasts swung free as bells,
and when I tipped the ancient waiter
he said, "Have a pleasant evening, folks,"
and I could see we had given him pleasure.

It could have been the fear of losing you
to Elizabeth, a hunchback from Bogota
whose scarlet fingernail you carried

like a love charm close to your heart in a
pocket of your stone-coloured overcoat.
It was lucky I knew, to touch a hunchback's
hump, to take on some of that
loneliness, but I'd never be a match

for Elizabeth who wrote poetry to you
in Spanish, poetry you told me
was untranslatable. My love, the words
I love you are words I'd recognize
in any language, no matter how foreign.
Or it could have been the fear of losing
myself in the wholeness of your body, as
back then, I believed it was.

These days my body is filled with a kind
of singing; I ask you not to think of pain
when you come to listen to me. Think
instead of the white air, the pure light
we breathed together on that distant morning
in Sudden Valley, how you stopped me
from speaking about the future back then,
as if any kind of love could fail.

DEPRESSION IN DEBRECEN

(Budapest Spring Festival, Hungary, 1993)

Leaving Budapest we pass rows of bruise-coloured
apartment blocks the communists left behind
and a cemetery full of half-dug graves, good
reasons, our interpreter says, to write poetry
about beauty also. The graves stare back
at us as a black train crosses our tracks,
grey faces against the windows blurred
like brushstrokes x-ing out the past.

When I was a child I collected stamps. I had
diamonds immortalizing dead poets, and triangles
with histories of love and heartbreak
that took up three or more spaces in the pages
allocated to Magyar Posta. I don't know
what became of my life, or my desire
to open to those pages and feel the tender
blurring world fall into focus for something
longer than a moment.

In my pocket I turn our room-key in my hand,
so heavy in the new morning it almost feels

weightless. Last night at the hotel, drunk
on Bull's Blood after a gypsy offered you sex
with a twist in the No Problem Drink Bar,
we fought and you threw my half-packed suitcase
after me as I tried to get away. It hit
the side of my head where memories are locked
and I went back through my life to a dimly lit
room, and my father with his belt the colour
of dark chocolate standing over me, bringing
the world down onto my head.

Our interpreter points to the slaughterhouse
where she once worked and fell in love
with an adulterer. Every day they went home
with blood on their hands, until he confessed.
She is frail and the bones beneath her
sunken face stick out like bones unearthed,
exposed to wind and rain, then buried again.
In Debrecen we drink rare brandy with local writers
and communicate through the only words we have
in common: man, conflict, depressio, migraine.

Attila, the poet, asks if I have a migraine
because I keep touching the hurt place
on the side of my head – "Beauty is only
skin deep," our fathers said, caressing the bruises

as if they, too, were blessings bestowed
upon us, blessings we were told to keep counting
every day and so we did. I counted the days
until my father went away for good, then stood
at his grave weeping half in love, half out
of rage. Feeling the raised flesh under

my fingers today, I think – this is my way
of keeping in touch with you, far away
to the south, as if hurt were a horizon
you could ever cross over. *"Mee-graine,"*
says Attila. *"Man. Conflict. Depressio."*

On the drive back to Budapest I rest
my forehead against the tinted window and watch
black rain beading in my reflection. Years ago
when first in love I would have compared
the streaking rain to tears, though I know better
now. Hungover at the hotel you will be dressing
for dinner in the suit you wore to our wedding
seven years ago, but I won't know what to expect
after so many years when I turn the key in the lock,
as if coming home again could ever be that simple.

Strange to be travelling back through
darkness, too, desiring everything I am

afraid of. Stranger still to centre longing
in the father of a child you will never be
sure of; one who looks back at you through a history
of love and heartbreak and who, without touching,
takes the weighted room-key from your hand.

LOVE, HE SAID

In Spain, sixteen years ago,
I sat under a twisted pear tree
writing doomed poetry.

At night I put on black
and went down into the peaceful village.

My eyes, he said, were like
terrifying raped blossoms.
I loved him because so much was always lost
in translation.

Love, he said, is taking a long time
always. In my room where we lay
for a small night above the peaceful village
I think, looking back, I understood him.

THE LONG WAY HOME

I rode through Paris once.
I was twenty-seven and I'd been
told all taxi-drivers were
untrustworthy, they'd take you
the long way home.

I did not know I was living my life then
for what I have become.

My driver got lost.
At least he said we were lost.
I didn't know the city
so I had to take his word for it.
We drove all night.

I had wanted to be a woman
who could make any man
remember how good it always was
how sweet and sad and good

but I'm only what I am

and I don't remember how the night
ended, or if I caught the
morning train

or if the man awaiting me
in Marseilles was sick with worry
when he met the morning train,
and how the children, if there were
children, kissed me in the rain.

It was the last time I got lost.
I remember how he looked at me
on those dark wide streets
so that I almost stopped doubting him

and later, in the narrow bed
how eager I was to prove I'd always
trusted him, when he said

show me, show me what a man is for

and I did.

CANADIAN ROULETTE

Let's not invent any more weapons.
Let's grope in the fog
wearing coarse wool underwear instead.
Let's be kind to one another
and let's not write any more hate poetry.

Let's pretend we're in love with one another.
You go first.

Acknowledgments

Many of the poems in this book have previously appeared, or will soon appear, in the following magazines and anthologies:

In Canada: *Anthos*; *Barbed Lyres* (Key Porter); *Beneath the Surface*; *Border Crossings*; *Brick*; *Canadian Literature*; *Canadian Poetry Review*; *The Canadian Women Writers Engagement Calendar 1986*; *The Dry Wells of India* (Harbour Publishing); *Event*; *Exile*; *Kitchen Talk* (Red Deer University Press); *The Malahat Review*; *The New Quarterly*; *Prism*; *Prison Journal*; *Quarry*; *The View from Here* (Nelson Canada); *Toronto Life*; *Writers' Quarterly*

In the U.S.A.: *Iris*; *Nimrod*; *Pivot*; *Prairie Schooner*; *The Southern Review*

In Australia: *Poetry Australia*

A number of these poems were published by Reference West in a chapbook entitled *In the Small Hours of the Rain*, which won the bp Nichol Poetry Chapbook Award for 1990.

The Spiritualization of Cruelty, a portfolio including six of my poems and drawings by Pavel Skalnik, was published as a limited, lettered and numbered edition, 1992, by Lake Gallery of Toronto.

Six poems were included in The Embalmer's Art: Selected and New published in 1991 by Exile. These poems, as they appear in this collection, have all been revised. My thanks to Stan Dragland for his unwavering eye.

Thanks, too, to Seán Virgo for his input over the years, and to Marilyn Bowering for the echo of her line, "love jumps away..." The last line of the title poem owes a debt to Robert Penn Warren.